Whispers of an Ordinary Life

PALLAVI MOHAPATRA

BookLeaf Publishing

India | USA | UK

Presentation by *BookLeaf Publishing*

Web: www.bookleafpub.com

E-mail: info@bookleafpub.com

ISBN:9789360943974

First edition 2024

DEDICATION

To my loving family for their continuous
support and encouragement. And my lovely
daughter who always amazes me with her 'new'
perspectives.

ACKNOWLEDGEMENT

I would like to thank BookLeaf Publishing for making this dream of publishing, the collection of my most cherished memories, come true. It's always the start that's the most daunting challenge but BookLeaf made it a lot easier as a shared journey.

PREFACE

I used to think the extraordinary was always somewhere out there—a distant mountain peak, a bustling foreign city, a whirlwind romance. But over time, I learnt that the most heartfelt wonders often hide in plain sight. It's the warmth of the morning sun on my skin, a stranger's unexpected smile, the quiet song of birds at dusk. "Whispers of an Ordinary Life" is a collection that seeks to resonate with readers who find wonder in the simple, the profound in the fleeting, and the universal within the deeply personal. It's an invitation to slow down, pay attention, and rediscover the magic that surrounds us every day.

My Universe folds into You!

The moon, a pearl on velvet skies,
Spills silver where the starlight lies.
And in this hush, this gentle night,
My heart finds peace, my soul takes flight.

The world melts down to just us two,
Grass damp with kisses of the dew.
Your hand in mine, a whispered vow,
Beneath the stars, in this timeless now.

The constellations paint the eternal vast,
Each flicker tells of moments passed.
But in your eyes, a brighter stream,
A future spun in starlit dreams.

No distant shores my heart would crave,
With you beside, the world's my wave.
For in this dew-kissed, moonlit space,
I find all wonders in your face.

The Rhythm of Nurture

I saw a dove, wings half-unfurled,
Not in flight, but warming her world.
Beneath her feathers, fledglings stirred,
Nurtured with whispers, love her word.

In every shielding, tender guise,
A mother's heart knows sacrifice.
Through sleet or storm, her watch remains,
While fledglings grow, find strength in veins.

The show of life, my child, must go on,
But joy and hardship walk as one.
Face the world with a lifted chin,
Each dark night yields where days begin.

Hold your spirit strong and bright,
Yet bend where sorrow takes its flight.
Oh, let your dreams touch boundless space,
And know I cheer you on in the race.

A Pause in the Chase

Today life's like an F1 race, everyone's running
at a frantic pace.
Saturation, recession and competition are all
over the place.
But hey, do pause, breathe deep and look up at
space!

Education, graduation, occupation leave nothing
to imagination,
Kids dread a lengthy essay at the end of a
vacation.
But hey, do sit back, toes in sand to enjoy the
changing season.

Money, energy, aspirations and ambitions galore,
No time to unwind and enjoy nature's grandeur.
But hey, do take a boat out and cast a line into
the river.

Satisfaction, salvation are the quest of the older
generation,
Who said they don't pine for a family
staycation?
Hey, make time for them cause they just need a
little attention.

Live the life from your childhood fascination,
Don't get tangled in the grown-up complication,
Hey, let smiles outnumber regrets when you near
the final destination!

A Shining Knight

Look up, look down, look left or right,
From every angle, the day shines bright.
Start your journey with a joyful knight,
And watch your path fill with pure delight!

Simply because we live with those who inspire,
Morning, noon, and through twilight's fire.
A firm support when days grow dire,
Soothing our spirit, lifting us higher.

May every soul find a North Star bright,
To chase off shadows with a guiding light.
A protector near, always in sight,
Our champion true, a steadfast knight.

Call him a hero, or love so right,
Vows set in stone, held ever so tight.
If fear or worry dims your inner light,
Remember, dear heart, a new path takes flight!

Coz we have a champion, with spirit so bright.

The Lady of the Mist

(Inspired by a drive through
Saputara on a rainy day)

Mist descends, a veil so light,
On peaks where clouds take playful flight.
The valley bursts into emerald green,
Where blossoms paint a vibrant scene.

A stream awakes with bubbling glee,
Its laughter echoes, wild and free.
While ancient trees stand tall and wise,
Their branches reaching for the skies.

The air hangs cool with drizzling rain,
Each drop a pearl on the windowpane.
And in this world of verdant dreams,
My spirit soars, my heart, it beams.

The mountains call, a whispered song,
Of earth's sweet rhythm, wild and strong.
Where nature paints with tender hand,
A timeless, mystique, ever-shifting land.

Seaside Symphony

(A sunset at a beach in south Goa)

Seabirds wheel and dip on high,
Their cries like laughter in the sky.
Dolphins arc with playful scheme,
Chasing sunlight in a liquid dream.

The ocean breathes, a rhythmic sigh,
Foamy whispers where seashells lie.
Sand crabs scurry, bold and fleet,
Tiny footprints etched in sand so sweet.

The breeze, it carries whispers low,
Of far-off lands where trade winds blow.
My hair a tangled, salty crown,
As sunlight casts its magic down.

The sunset paints with fiery hand,
Orange and crimson, sea and sand.
Colours melt to twilight's grace,
As the sky turns a jewelled space.

Stars like diamonds dust the night,
The moon's silver rays bring soft light.
The gentle tide, a sweet caress,
Calming the mind, soothing stress.

Bioluminescent sparks ignite,
Dancing where the waves take flight.
The white sand, slipping under my feet,
As time slows down into a soft retreat.

My heart finds peace upon this shore,
Where ocean's soul does rise and soar.
Each breath a balm, each moment free,
The beach, the waves, just sing to me.

My spirit rests in this embrace,
As worries fade without a trace.
The ocean's pulse becomes my own,
Where peace resides, and I am home.

Secret Admiration

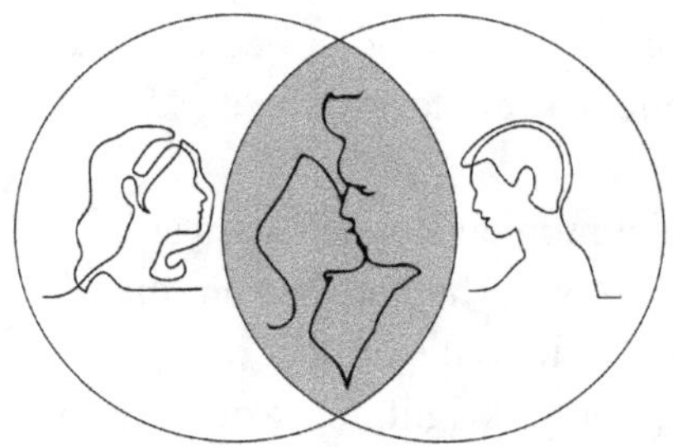

Your eyes hold secrets, depths untold,
A story whispered, yet to unfold.
Each radiant smile, a puzzle bright,
My mind unravels, day and night.

Your laughter echoes, a melody sweet,
A rhythm my heart can barely meet.
Each word you speak, a treasured sound,
My spirit soars, no longer ground.

You walk with grace, an air so rare,
A world apart, beyond compare.
My heart admires from a distance wide,
Adoring you, with nothing left to hide.

Your voice, like breeze on a misty morn,
Whispers of a world where dreams are born.
I long to know the thoughts you hold,
The mysteries your soul might unfold.

I wonder if your thoughts might stray,
To me, a shadow by the way.
Do I cross your mind, a fleeting spark,
Or fade unseen, lost in the dark?

In quiet moments, when stars shine,
I dare to wish that you were mine.
But like a moonbeam, out of reach,
You shine so bright, my words lose speech.

Although you seem a distant star,
My heart won't stray, won't travel far.
Each thought of you, a sweet delight,
The mystery lingers, day and night.

Could I ever be worthy in your sight,
Or am I bound to watch your light?
To catch a glimpse of who you are,
A radiant beacon, guiding star.

Though leagues divide us, I'll confess,
This foolish heart holds nothing less
Than pure devotion, true and deep,
An admiration my soul will always keep.

Perhaps one day the stars will turn,
And in your gaze, my name you'll learn.
Until that moment, dreams suffice,
Of you, my wonder, my paradise.

Remember when....

The thread that bound us, once so strong,
Seems frayed and tangled in this song.
We built a world, a lovely place,
With whispered jokes and laughter's grace.

From being my shield to the tears you dried,
A constant by my side, in you I did confide.
Through mischiefs managed and battles won,
You were my bestie, second to none.

The miles they stretch, a cruel divide,
The laughters echo, deep inside.
I long to rewind, to simpler days,
To be as carefree in youthful daze.

Though paths may diverge, and seasons change,
The bond we forged, it won't rearrange.
You're more than just a memory's hold,
A friendship's ember, warm and bold.

I wish I could be your shield once more,
Deflect the blows life has in store.
Know that across the miles so wide,
My thoughts are with you, my friend, my guide.

Though whispers fade, and silence grows,
The love we shared, forever flows.
And when the stars align just right,
I look forward to the day we'll reunite.

Paragliding Adventure

The world shrinks down, a distant scene unfurled,
As I take off, a thrilling dream tightly swirled.

Himalayan peaks, their icy white a blinding flash,
Sparkle below my daring flight, a titan's mighty clash.

Verdant valleys stretch so wide, a tapestry of green,
Where eagles ride the windswept heights, a fierce and noble queen.

The frigid air upon my face, a kiss of freedom's might,
A rush of wind, a fearless embrace, where shadows are not in sight.

Treacherous cliffs, their edges sharp, cloud the
mind with awe,
Fill me with wonder, leave their mark where my
senses start to thaw.

Exhilaration courses through, a wild and surging
tide,
As fear and wonder mix anew, a battle deep
inside.

This bird's-eye view, so wild and vast, a canvas
painted wide,
Each moment fleeting, flying past where dreams
and fears collide.

My spirit soars above it all, where earthly
bounds unwind,
In this dance where I might fall, but a bolder self
I find.

And liberation lights my way, its beacon shining
bright,
The cost of freedom I gladly pay, in this
breathtaking flight.

For in this flight, so bold and grand, horizons
stretch so far,
I conquer fear, touch the distant land, a fearless
shooting star.

Kerala Dreams

Palm fronds sway in gentle breeze,
Sunlight streaming through the trees.
The houseboat glides, a tranquil dream,
Upon the backwater's mirrored beam.

A kingfisher, in jewelled flight,
Skims the water, a dazzling sight.
Lotuses bloom, soft and serene,
Their petals paint a vibrant scene.

Villages nestle by the shore,
Life's rhythm echoes, evermore.
The scent of spices fills the air,
As flavours mingle, rich and rare.

Time seems to drift at a gentle pace,
The mind wanders in poignant grace,
The water's rhythm soothes my soul,
A journey where I feel made whole.

Sunset paints a golden hue,
Across the sky, so vast and true.
Stars emerge, a shimmering guide,
As fireflies dance at the waterside.

The houseboat halts, a peaceful nest,
Where dreams unfold, and spirits rest.
This backwater haven, sweet and slow,
A place where hearts and memories grow.

A Painted Sunrise

A jolly stream wrapped in a blanket of mist,
Gurgling down the verdant mountain pass,
The ember sky, oh so sun-kissed,
Turns into a brightly painted canvas.

Birdsong trills, a symphony so bright,
Whispers of dawn erase the night.
Hills unfold in lush and rolling green,
Tea gardens stretch, a patchwork scene.

The mist begins its gentle dance and sway,
Sunlight peeks, and shadows melt away.
Munnar wakes to greet the golden morn,
Where every breath feels fresh and newborn.

In this sweet hour, as light begins to stream,
A sense of peace descends, a blissful dream.
The valley smiles, a vibrant, living art,
And the morning sight warms the very heart.

Golden Hour by the Sea

Crystal waters shine and shiver,
Reflecting sunset's golden quiver.
No soft sand, but rocks and shell,
Where ocean whispers weave their spell.

The sun descends, a blazing sphere,
Painting waves with hues so dear.
Tourists flock, with laughter bright,
Seeking solace in the fading light.

A dip to cool the sun-kissed skin,
Where gentle waves wash worries thin.
The joyous cries of children rise,
Mirroring seagulls in the painted skies.

Vendors call with tempting fares,
Ice cream sweet and crisp that snares.
Hot tea warms against the evening breeze,
As colours fade with gentle ease.

The sun dips low, a fiery crown,
Sinking slow where sea meets the town.
Kanyakumari's magic seems,
A sunset woven into dreams.

Where Rivers and Oceans Meet

Aboard a shikara, gently we glide,
Through serpentine canals, where secrets hide.
Poovar's backwaters, a mirrored sheen,
Mangrove sentinels, a vibrant screen.

Sunlight dapples, a speckled delight,
On leaves that whisper in the morning's light.
Twigs entwined, a nature's embrace,
A silent symphony, in this hidden space.

The river unfolds, a turquoise surprise,
Where meeting the sea, a new wonder lies.
Poovar's beach stretches, a canvas so grand,
White sands whisper, waves crash on the land.

Green and blue waters, a mesmerizing blend,
Nature's masterpiece, that knows no end.
The deep sea roars, a symphony bold,
A tale of power, yet a story untold.

From tranquil backwaters, to ocean's embrace,
Poovar's beauty, leaves an enchanting trace.
A shikara's journey, a memory to hold,
Of a land where serenity, unfolds and unfolds.

The Heart Goes On....

On a land deserted and lone,
Memories insanely hunt in vain,
Stances of joy, stances of pain,
And down the lane, the heart goes on.

Shadows flutter past in a trance,
Across mirages of luck and chance,
Weighing the cons of a futile run,
And down the lane, the heart goes on.

A hope, a faith, a longing desire,
Buried in the war of biggest share,
Shrieks and cries with the wind gone,
And down the lane, the heart goes on.

Still wandering for that love so pure,
A divine touch only peace can assure,
To heal the wound and soothe the burn,
And down the lane, the heart goes on.

Dreams the soul, dreams mankind,
Let forever the heart rule the mind,
The waves of hope crash and return,
As down the lane, the heart goes on.

An effort neither insane nor in vain,
Links the world in a golden chain,
Spreading love, love and love alone,
Down the lane, the heart goes on.

(It's true that the mind is the think-tank,
But at times let the heart think.
The mind can become selfish
But the heart is as selfless as the earth—a true
heart that is true to the Divine!)

My Little World

Oh, how beautiful is my little world
Studded with rubies and emerald.
And there's an angel who takes its care,
Flooding it with things wonderful and rare.

Sunlight spills like golden beams,
Nurturing hopes and weaving dreams.
Laughter echoes, a joyful chime,
Marking moments both sweet and sublime.

Whispers of love paint gentle streaks,
Across rosy smiles and tender cheeks.
Kindness blossoms with radiant might,
Guiding steps through the darkest of night.

Oh, my world, though small it may seem,
Holds treasures beyond the wildest dream.
With an angel's touch and love so bright,
My heart soars free, with surging delight.

Adventures await, with stories to share,
And challenges too, with lessons to bear.
But no matter the trials, my heart won't break,
For in this world, resilience I'll make.

Through thick and thin, through life's every
bend,
My angel stands beside me, until the very end.
And for all the blessings, both big and small,
My grateful heart finds wonder in it all.

The Lost Castle

Lost in an ocean of gloom and despair,
My heart aches, questioning why fate did
conspire,
Robbing me of simple, cherished pleasures,
Treasures my wounded soul so desires.

Guilt whispers in a voice too near,
My eyes brim with a mournful tear.
Whose fault was it? Answers unclear,
But the pain I bear feels far too severe.

The past has slipped beyond my grasp,
Consequences loom, their shadows cast.
Alone, perhaps, with burdens to bear,
A futile fight against a world unfair.

Yet, wait! A flicker of hope remains,
If I seize the chance, break free from my chains.
With strength and resolve, a lifeline I'll weave,
A rope of hope, if only I believe.

Life's a vibrant dream, so I've been told,
With highs and lows, a tale to unfold.
Like a stream, I'll brave the turbulent flow,
Carving a path through the unknown, I'll grow.

A beckoning call, a promise so bright,
"Don't waste a moment, reclaim what's your
right!"
The opportunity shimmers, its time has begun,
This life is mine, a battle to be won.

The castle of hope, my heart's sole desire,
A goal unyielding, fuelling my inner fire.
Against a twilight sky, its silhouette gleams,
That lost domain, the heart of my dreams.

Birds of Joy

With the first rays of the sun,
Night's hushed silence is broken,
A symphony of joy has begun,
Sweet melodies by wings awoken.

Feathers flash with colours bright,
Tiny jewels against the morning light.
Their chorus fills the waking air,
A celebration free of every care.

Treetops sway to their merry tune,
As sunlight melts away the moon.
The world below hears their refrain,
And hearts awaken, joy unchained.

Sparrows chirp and robins call,
Melodies mingle, both large and small.
From leafy branches to rooftops high,
Their music paints the morning sky.

Sleepy eyes flutter open and beam,
As the world awakens from its tranquil dream.
A smile graces every face they meet,
Inspired by the songbirds' chorus so sweet.

Worries fade with each lilting note,
And spirits rise, on wings afloat.
The birdsong's symphony, a joyous decree,
Unleashing the light that longs to be free.

The Earth's Relief

Clouds like swollen sails, they tear and spill,
Tiny crystal raindrops start to thrill.

Summer's heat retreats in haste,
The thirsty earth begins to taste.

Soil drinks deep, a gasp of sweet relief,
Releasing scents once held in parched belief.

Lost greenery unfurls with vibrant might,
Earth's velvet cloak awakens in the light.

Ponds and rivers swell, their waters gleam,
Frolicking frogs create a joyous team.

Wildflowers paint the fields in colours bright,
Beckoning butterflies in dazzling flight.

A wave of cheer sweeps through the land,
Nature's glory, a sight so grand.

The peacock's feathers, a vibrant display,
Celebrate rain that washes woes away.

Thunder booms, and lightning flashes free,
A cleansing storm, a wild symphony!

More than mother, more than child!

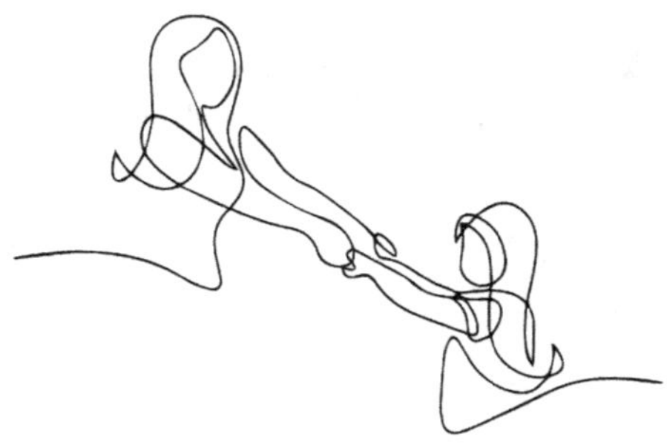

The first touch, a world shifts and aligns,
A tiny life, warm within these arms of mine.
Paper napkin size, a wiggling form I hold,
Beady eyes, black hair—a miracle to unfold.

Nine months within, a bond both felt and
unseen,
But holding her, it bursts, this joy so keen.
That tiny face with trusting smile so bright,
Shifted my world, cast a whole new light.

Today I glance back, at that moment so dear,
And trace the path we've walked, year after year.
Learning to parent, with falters and might,
Balancing softness, and life lessons that guide.

Frustrations may build, like a gathering storm,
But her peaceful sleep, my heart it does reform.

A troubled mind finds solace in her embrace,
Her simple hug, a love that fills this space.

She sees me as magic, a solver of every ill,
And that sweet faith, it fuels my determined
will.
A decade's walk, as mother, as friend, by her
side,
More lessons I've learned, child, than I could
provide.

A Slice of Life

T'was a milestone, standing at life's most
decisive turn,
Not many knew, to be engineers we were born.
To colour our dreams, from night to morn,
Into the KIIT university, we were sworn.

Anxious faces, twinkling eyes, a pounding heart,
Excitement high, as our careers made a kickstart.
As days passed, onward and forward we did
dart,
To emerge as youths knowledgeable and smart.

Welcomed we were, into this family, with
grandeur,
And we did keep up the trend for sure.
Slowly and steadily, pop a magic did conjure,
That turned strangers into bosom pals and more.

The peerless symphony basked in ardent
harmony,
It made even the routine free from monotony.
Cradled in efficient hands, learning was joy not
agony,
As we trained to face life's challenging
cacophony.

Colourful 'Vibranzs', rocking star nights, days of
frolic and fun,
Moments of triumph, moments of tears, in one
thread were spun.
Those mischiefs and pranks, a get-set-go and
run,
Filled the days, weaving the most wondrous ever
pun.

As time does, stealthily it hopped and flew,
Sculpting mature graduates, even before we
knew.
With manifold opportunities and education,
blessed are few,
Strengthening us as we prepared to enter a world
new.

Bonds forged in these jolly years, for a lifelong
do remain,
With a promise to stand by each other—be it sun
or rain.

Aspiring for a good life laced with success and
splendid gain,
Friends parted, longingly looking forward to
meet again.

A Dancer's Triumph

On stage she stands, a vision bright,
My daughter, bathed in golden light.
Her yellow saree, a sunlit delight,
Sparkles with jewels that banish the night.

Like porcelain, flawless and serene,
A blossom rare, full of sheen.
Her hands, like birds, take flight and fold,
A story whispered, ages old.

Each step, a fleeting beat on the floor,
Emotions bloom, and feelings soar.
Eyes downcast, then a playful glance,
The jasmine offered, a sacred trance.

To Krishna's form, her heart takes flight,
A love divine, a radiant light.
My breath I hold, spellbound, I stare,
The goddess dancing, free of care.

No hint of fear, a stage possessed,
Her passion burning, hearts impressed.
Her tiny frame, a powerhouse strong,
A melody in motion, flowing along.

With every gesture, my pride takes wing,
My little girl, a wondrous thing.
She owns the stage, her spirit bold,
Swirling and gliding with graceful hold.